Easy MathART Projects and Activities

By Cecilia Dinio-Durkin

SCHOLASTIC
PROFESSIONAL BOOKS

NEW YORK • TORONTO • LONDON • AUCKLAND • SYDNEY
MEXICO CITY • NEW DELHI • HONG KONG

I'd very much like to acknowledge all the wonderful suggestions, encouragement, and ideas my editor, Deborah Schecter, gave me in writing this book, as well as my other Scholastic Professional Books.

Front cover and interior design by Kathy Massaro
Cover photos by Donnelly Marks
Interior photographs by Donnelly Marks and Sal Principato
Interior illustrations by Kate Flanagan with additional illustrations by James Graham Hale

ISBN # 0-590-37896-1
Copyright © 1999 by Cecilia Dinio-Durkin

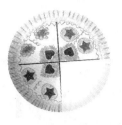

Contents

Math is found in the most basic of art concepts. From geometric shapes to the patterns of colors—math is everywhere. And what better way to bring math skills and concepts to life for young children than with art!

In *Easy MathART Projects and Activities*, children create wonderful art projects—all based on math skills that correlate with the standards recommended by the National Council of Teachers of Mathematics. (See Connections With the NCTM Standards chart, page 6.) Whether you're making Count-Up Birthday Candle Cards, Harvest Corncob Patterns, or Heart-Filled Valentines, the activities and projects in this book will enable you to combine art with math lessons all year long. No matter the level of math or talent in art, every child in your class will learn—and produce beautiful and festive decorations and gifts at the same time!

Each project focuses on a specific math skill or concept and includes a complete list of materials, grouping suggestions, step-by-step instructions, teaching tips, and ideas for seasonal or holiday tie-ins. You'll also find reproducible patterns and worksheets, Variations—ideas for altering the basic projects, and More Math extension ideas. Book Gallery recommends books to share with your class that relate to the lesson's math concept or holiday tie-in.

I hope that you and your class enjoy these explorations in math and art. Who knows?—you may inspire a budding Michelangelo or Leonardo da Vinci—both great artists who used math in their work!

— *Cecilia Dinio-Durkin*

Tips for Using This Book

❁ Before you do a project with children, make it yourself. This will enable you to determine how much time you'll need and what adaptations you may want to make.

❁ Provide lunch trays to help contain children's work space. On trays, little pieces stay close by and spills can be easily wiped clean and dry. If a particular project involves several materials, hand them out as needed during the course of the project.

❁ Most of the projects in this book use everyday items that you probably already have in your kitchen or closet. Other materials can be found at most grocery or arts and crafts stores. Feel free to make substitutions or changes to any of the projects.

❁ Many of the activities suggest having children write or draw responses in a math journal. A math journal can be a looseleaf notebook or sheets of paper, folded and stapled together. Math entries can be as simple as recording an estimate before discovering the answer, or as complex as writing an explanation of a math concept or skill. You may suggest that children write or draw in their journals every day, once a week, or as each new concept or skill is learned—it's up to you. No matter how you use them, journals are a valuable tool that display children's progress and give you insights into their thinking.

✿ Continue to reinforce concepts by using the projects in this book again and again. Alter a project's seasonal connection and you'll have a new lesson! (You'll find suggestions for doing this in Variations.) Make a skill more challenging by adding more elements, and you'll have a math extension. Keep children's creative juices flowing, building their math skills as you build on these art projects.

✿ Celebrate the Math–Art connection by setting up an area or bulletin board to display children's projects. This will help children take pride in their accomplishments and will provide you with an attractive and ever-evolving reference point for reviewing math concepts.

Display Ideas

To enhance some of the projects in this book, you may want to have your class make these simple and decorative frames. They are fun to make and let children explore geometric shapes.

Craft-Stick Frames

Glue craft sticks together to make frames in various geometric shapes, such as triangles, squares, and rectangles. The sticks can be painted, wrapped in ribbon or pipe cleaners, or decorated by gluing on beans, beads, buttons, tissue paper, or fabric.

Paper-Plate Frames

Cut out the center of a paper plate and use it as a frame. Color or decorate the rim, as described for the craft-stick frames.

Acetate Accent Frames

Sandwich a picture between two pieces of acetate, and seal the edges by gluing on ribbon or construction paper or using colored tape. You could also punch holes along the sides and give children yarn or ribbon to "sew" a frame together.

Corrugated Cardboard Frames

This frame is too difficult for children to make, but it is a great way to make large frames. Use a sharp knife to cut up old boxes. Peel away the outer layer of the cardboard to make a textured finish. Or leave the outer layer to paint, color with markers or crayons, or cover with fabric or contact paper.

Connections With the NCTM Standards

	Mathematics as Problem Solving	Mathematics as Communication	Mathematics as Reasoning	Mathematical Connections	Estimation	Number Sense and Numeration	Concepts of Whole Number Operations	Whole Number Computation	Geometry and Spatial Sense	Measurement	Statistics and Probability	Fractions and Decimals	Patterns and Relationships
Number Art Posters	✳	✳	✳	✳		✳							✳
Natural Number Sun-Catchers	✳	✳	✳	✳		✳			✳				✳
Count-Up Birthday Candle Cards	✳	✳	✳	✳		✳							
New Year Countdown Crackers	✳	✳	✳	✳		✳	✳		✳		✳		
Paint-by-Number Pictures	✳	✳	✳	✳		✳							
Add-Up Family Portraits	✳	✳	✳	✳		✳	✳	✳					
Soapy Fraction Sculptures	✳	✳	✳	✳	✳	✳				✳		✳	✳
Fraction Subtraction Pies	✳	✳	✳	✳		✳	✳	✳				✳	
Snapshot Shape Frames	✳	✳	✳	✳					✳				
3-D Kiss-mas Ornaments	✳	✳	✳	✳	✳				✳	✳			
Heart-Filled Valentines	✳	✳	✳	✳	✳	✳	✳			✳			
Pipe-Cleaner Pals	✳	✳	✳	✳	✳			✳	✳		✳	✳	
Cuckoo Clocksicles	✳	✳	✳	✳		✳					✳		✳
Tooth Fairy Money-Tree Wheels	✳	✳	✳	✳		✳	✳	✳			✳		✳
Harvest Corncob Patterns	✳	✳	✳	✳									✳
Holiday Pattern Wreaths	✳	✳	✳	✳									✳
Costume-Combo Flip Books	✳	✳	✳	✳									✳

Number Art Posters

These beautiful posters show off children's number-writing skills.

For each child:

✿ Number Art Poster, pages 9–10
✿ scissors
✿ tape
✿ thin and thick markers, crayons, colored pencils

1 Begin by showing children examples of numbers and letters that have been designed in different ways in books, on packages, or on a computer. Talk with them about ways artists make numbers and letters look interesting and beautiful. Explain that artists do this by painting, drawing, or photographing them in different ways. Tell your class that they are going to be artists who design numbers.

2 Give each child copies of the Number Art Poster pages, tape, scissors, and markers, crayons, or colored pencils.

3 Have children cut out the poster pages along the heavy dotted lines and then line them up vertically and tape together, end to end. Tell children to fill in the numbers 1 to 10 on the poster. Encourage them to use the art materials to create different effects.

4 Ask children to create their own 1 to 10 number art in the blank columns on their poster.

5 Let children decorate the poster by coloring in the numbered boxes. Invite them to use different colors to make different patterns. They might decorate the empty spaces in the boxes with unusual shapes, squiggles, lines, dots, and so on. Display children's posters on a Number Art Poster Display.

To give children an example of creative graphic design in letters, refer to *The Graphic Alphabet* by David Pelletier (Orchard Books, 1996). Invite children to use the ideas in this book to inspire them as they design their numbers.

✿

From one gnu to ten lizards, children count up critters in the colorful and delightful book *Count* by Denise Fleming (Henry Holt, 1992).

✿

In *Feast for Ten* by Cathryn Falwell (Clarion, 1993), another lively counting book, young readers count to ten as they follow an African American family who go shopping and then prepare a meal.

Variation

Instead of having each child decorate a page of numbers from 1 to 10, create a class mural.

✿ Assign each child a number between 1 and 10. Ask children to write their number on the paper and decorate it however they wish.

✿ Invite children to help you hang the numbers in order or in some other number pattern on a bulletin board.

✿ Expand the number posters beyond 10 as children learn to write more numbers.

Number Art Poster

Tape Here

Number Art Poster

6 6 6

7 7 7

8 8 8

9 9 9

10 10 10

Easy MathART Projects and Activities   Scholastic Professional Books

Natural Number Sun-Catchers

Using things found in nature, children create number sun-catchers.

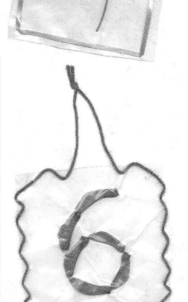

Materials

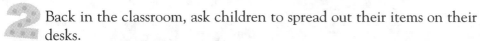

For each child:

❁ paper lunch bag
❁ natural objects from outdoors (leaves, twigs, seeds, pebbles)
❁ two 6- by 6-inch contact paper squares with backing attached
❁ scissors
❁ tape in different colors, construction paper strips, or ribbon for decorating
❁ hole punch and stapler
❁ yarn or raffia for hanging the sun-catchers

1 Take the class outside to collect things from nature. Talk to your class about the importance of being gentle to and respectful of trees, flowers, and all creatures. Tell children to pick up interesting items—fallen leaves, twigs, pebbles, and other natural things that they find on the ground. Give each child a paper bag for holding his or her finds.

2 Back in the classroom, ask children to spread out their items on their desks.

3 Explain that they will make a number sun-catcher, using the items they gathered outside. Give each child a square of contact paper with the backing still attached. Ask children to use the natural items to form a number on the contact paper. For example: a "1" could be made using a twig; a "2" could be made by bending two pieces of grass. Children may mix pebbles with pine needles, in whatever combination they choose.

4 Assign a number between 1 and 10 to each child, or let children choose a number they would like to make. Once children have their number and have chosen the objects they will use to make it, have them peel the backing from the contact paper. (Children may need help doing this.) Then have them place their objects, in the shape of their number, on the sticky side of the contact paper.

If possible, collect things after rainy or windy weather, when items such as leaves and twigs may have fallen to the ground. Let these materials dry completely before sealing between the contact paper squares.

Book Gallery

Before you begin your natural scavenger hunt, read *Anna's Garden Songs* by Mary O. Steele (Greenwillow, 1989). This book is sure to give children an appreciation for things that grow.

❀

After making their sun-catchers, children will enjoy listening to *Counting on the Woods* by George Ella Lyon (Dorling Kindersley, 1998). This delightful counting book, written as a poem, uses things in nature to count from 1 to 10.

❀

To bring out the concept of increasing numbers in nature and in daily life, share *Anno's Counting Book* by Mitsumasa Anno (Crowell, 1977).

❀

Suse McDonald and Bill Oakes create a parade of animals made up of numbers in *Puzzlers* (Dial, 1989).

5 Give children a second square of contact paper and have them peel off the backing and place the sticky side on top of their design. (Assist children who may need help lining up the two sheets.) Let children trim the edges if the sheets don't line up perfectly.

6 Show children how to use decorative tape to reinforce the edges, or staple construction paper strips around the square. Another option is to punch holes around the square and thread ribbon through the holes.

7 Punch a hole in the top of each sun-catcher and use string or raffia and tape to hang the numbers in a window. Then wait for the sun to shine in!

Variations

❀ If you don't assign numbers, let children put the numbers in order. Explain that they will place the sun-catchers in the window in order, from smallest to largest. Pick a child with a "1" sun-catcher. Show the child where the first sun-catcher will go. Have children raise their hands if they think they are next. Or call on children and ask them to put their number before or after the numbers already displayed.

❀ Let children use the number sun-catchers to do simple addition or subtraction problems.

More Math!

Number Rubs Go on a scavenger hunt around your school and the neighborhood in search of numbers. Provide children with 3- by 5-inch pieces of tracing paper and a crayon stripped of its outer covering. Once children have found a number that is raised or textured, show them how to lay the tracing paper over the number and rub firmly, using the length, not the tip, of the crayon. Frame the number rubs using one of the frames described on page 5. As a class, hang the numbers in order from smallest to largest around your classroom.

Count-Up Birthday Candle Cards

Children practice counting to make a birthday card that will light up a friend's special day.

Materials

For each child:

❀ Birthday Candle Card patterns, pages 14–15
❀ small, wrapped rolls of candy such as Smarties or miniature Tootsie Rolls (number of pieces will vary)
❀ half of a recycled file folder (see Ahead of Time below)
❀ scissors
❀ glue stick and white glue
❀ crayons, markers, paints, glitter, and glue (for decorating the card)

Ahead of Time

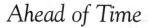

Cut the file folders in half as shown so that each side has a folded edge on the left. Each file folder will make two cards.

1 Hand out the two patterns to each child. Have children cut them out and decorate them with crayons or colored pencils.

2 Give each child one of the half-folders and a glue stick. Tell children to glue the cake pattern to the front of the folder. The fold should be on the left-hand side. Then have them glue the card's greeting inside the folder.

To foster the idea of giving, read *A Birthday for Frances* by Russell Hoban (Harper Trophy, 1994). In this story, Frances wrestles with the temptation to keep the candy she bought for her sister's birthday.

❁

Read aloud *The Day You Were Born* by Debra Frasier (Harcourt Brace, 1991). This beautifully written book will help each child feel all the more special for being here on Earth.

3 Ask children to decide for whom they wish to make a card, perhaps a friend or a sibling. Then ask: "How many candles will you need to show this person's age?"

4 Pass out the candies, letting children take the number of pieces they need to complete their card.

5 Let children use white glue to attach the candy candles to the top of the cake. When the glue is completely dry, let them fill in the inside of the card: write a greeting, fill in the total number of candles, and sign it.

6 Invite children to make the card more colorful and festive, using crayons, markers, paint, or glitter and glue.

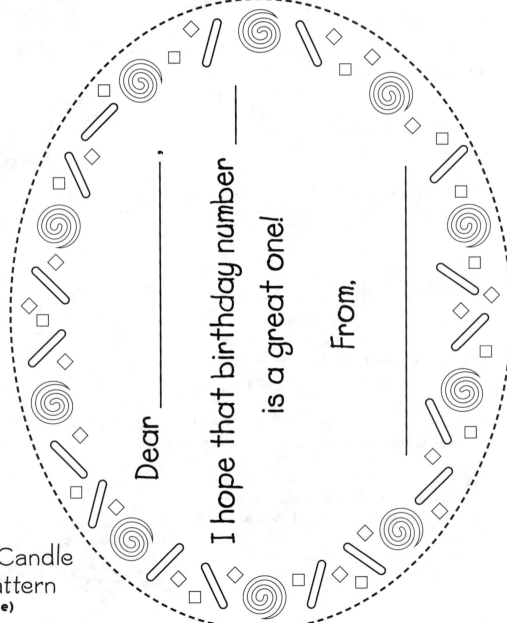

Dear

I hope that birthday number ___ is a great one!

From,

Birthday Candle Card Pattern
(Inside)

Birthday Candle Card Pattern
(Outside)

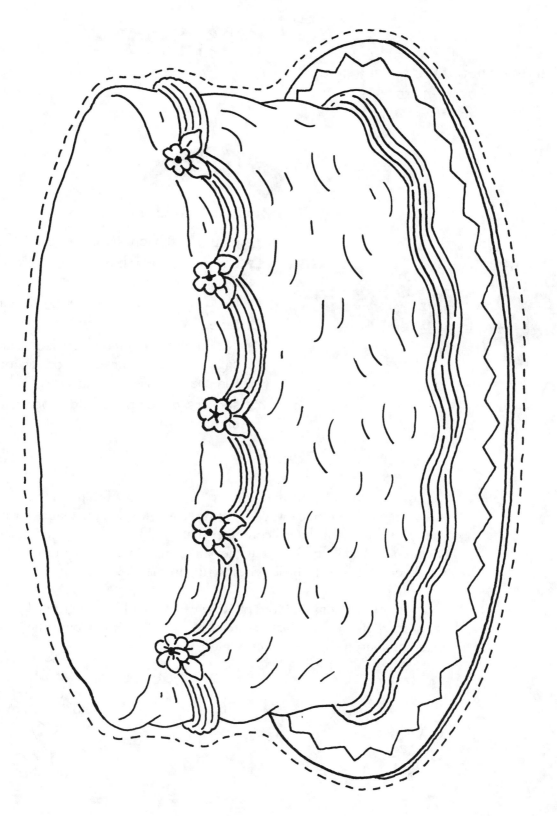

New Year Countdown Crackers

Children count to 10 as they fill up colorful countdown crackers to ring in the New Year!

Materials

For each child:

* empty bathroom-tissue tube
* two 5- by 10-inch pieces of colored tissue paper
* two 6-inch pieces of curling ribbon
* tape
* basket filled with small trinkets: stickers, small pieces of wrapped candy, balloons, fun-shaped erasers, etc. (for each group)
* stickers, glitter, paint, and other decorating materials

Making the Crackers

1 Explain to children what holiday "crackers" are. Tell them that they are an old-fashioned way of sharing small gifts. People long ago would pack gifts into a roll-shaped container that would make a popping sound when opened. Tell children that they are going to make Countdown Crackers filled with 10 little prizes to ring in the New Year.

2 List a few combinations of 10 prizes that children might pick to place in their crackers. List the items in equation form. Count the items to reinforce counting to 10. For example:

3 + **3** + **3** + **1** = **10**

3 Divide the class into groups and place baskets filled with various trinkets on each group's table. Let children each pick 10 prizes from the baskets.

4 Give each child the materials needed to construct the cracker (a bathroom-tissue tube, two pieces of colored tissue, and two pieces of curling ribbon). Have tape available as well. Show children how to loosely roll up the trinkets in one piece of tissue paper, securing the ends by gently twisting them closed.

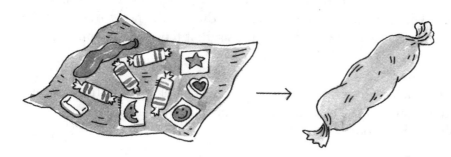

5 Have children place the tissue-filled packets into the center of the bathroom tissue tube. Children may need help positioning the packet so that an equal amount of tissue paper sticks out of each end of the roll.

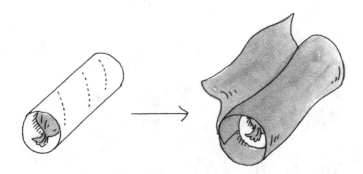

6 Show children how to roll the tube inside the second piece of tissue paper and tape it closed.

7 Tell children to use the curling ribbon to tie closed each end of the cracker. (To make the crackers look extra festive, help children use scissors to curl the ribbon.)

8 Let children decorate the outside of the tube with stickers, glitter, paint, or other decorating materials.

Book Gallery

Happy New Year! by Emery Bernhard (Lodestar Books, 1996) explains the history of the holiday and describes the New Year traditions celebrated by people around the world, today and long ago.

❀

Through simple, bold illustrations, *Twelve Ways to Get to 11* by Eve Merriam (Simon & Schuster, 1993) shows 12 different groupings of common objects, such as popcorn and peanut shells, that add up to 11.

Popping Open the Crackers

1 Bring in the New Year with a bang! Collect the crackers in a basket. Then have children pick a cracker other than the one they made.

2 To open the crackers, tell children to pull on both ends of the tissue paper. Have each child count the prizes in the cracker.

3 Ask for volunteers to count aloud, one by one, the prizes in their cracker. Then ask them to group together all the prizes that are alike and to write on the chalkboard an equation that represents them.

4 Ask each child to describe the combination of prizes in the cracker they picked. List the combinations on the chalkboard. Discuss other possible combinations.

5 Let children record the contents of their crackers in their math journals in equation form. For example: $3 + 3 + 2 + 2 = 10$.

More Math!

Shape Crackers Have children fill their tube with objects that represent a shape you assign, such as a triangle, square, or circle. Ask them to look for the shape in magazine pictures that they can cut out, stamps, stickers, candy, and so on. Ask children to open the crackers and identify the shape found inside.

Statistics Crackers Have children pick a number between 1 and 10 and then fill the tube with that number of items. Children can then exchange crackers and open them. Say the numbers 1 to 10 aloud, and ask children to raise their hands when you call out the number represented by their cracker. Make a chart of the results. Help children make inferences from the data. Which number was picked most often? Least often?

Paint-by-Number Pictures

Children add and subtract to create colorful paint-by-number pictures.

Materials

For each child:

❀ Paint-by-Number Addition or Paint-by-Number Subtraction pattern, pages 20–21

❀ pencil

❀ markers, crayons, or paint and paintbrushes

1 Give each child a copy of the Paint-by-Number Addition page or the Paint-by-Number Subtraction page. Tell children to solve the problems and write them inside each of the spaces.

2 Explain to children how to use the color key. Children match each answer with the numbers on the key, then paint or color the spaces as indicated.

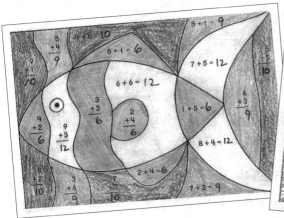
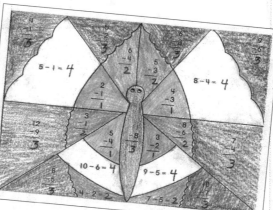

Variation

❀ Make your own paint-by-number pictures. Make copies of coloring book pages and assign each space a color. Write a key for the answers and the colors. Then make up addition and subtraction problems for each space.

Book Gallery

For more addition and subtraction fun, share *The Addition Wipe-Off Book* and *The Subtraction Wipe-Off Book* by Alan Hartley (Scholastic, 1988). Children will enjoy using these books again and again.

❀

Young readers get to add and subtract when the circus comes to town In *Number One, Number Fun* by Kay Chorao (Holiday House, 1995). They'll also adore adding and subtracting coral reef sea creatures in Joy N. Hulme's *Sea Sums* (Hyperion, 1996).

Paint-by-Number Addition

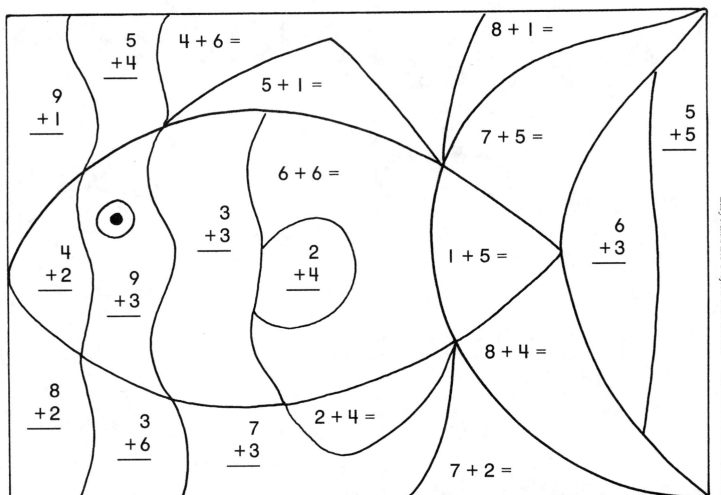

Easy Math ART Projects and Activities   Scholastic Professional Books

If the answer is	Color the space
6	Red
9	Green
10	Blue
12	Yellow

Color Key

Paint-by-Number Subtraction

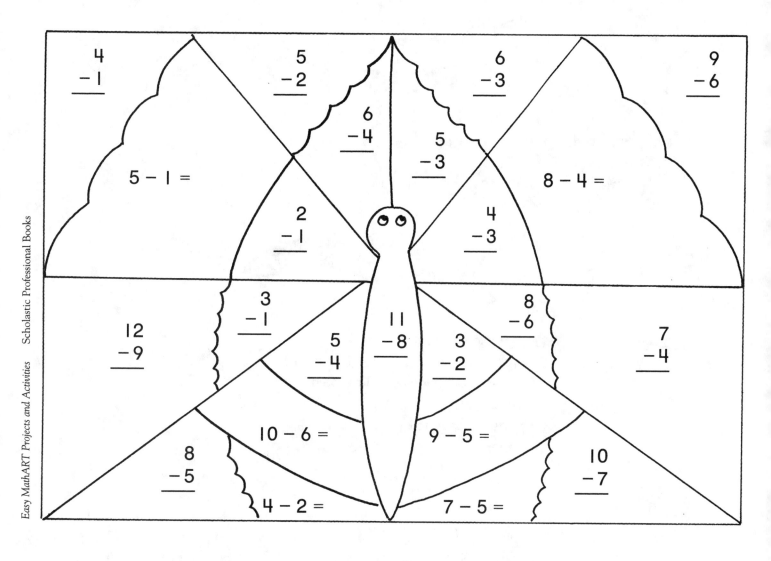

$$\begin{array}{r} 4 \\ -1 \\ \hline \end{array}$$

$$\begin{array}{r} 5 \\ -2 \\ \hline \end{array}$$

$$\begin{array}{r} 6 \\ -3 \\ \hline \end{array}$$

$$\begin{array}{r} 9 \\ -6 \\ \hline \end{array}$$

$$\begin{array}{r} 6 \\ -4 \\ \hline \end{array}$$

5 − 1 =

$$\begin{array}{r} 5 \\ -3 \\ \hline \end{array}$$

8 − 4 =

$$\begin{array}{r} 2 \\ -1 \\ \hline \end{array}$$

$$\begin{array}{r} 4 \\ -3 \\ \hline \end{array}$$

$$\begin{array}{r} 12 \\ -9 \\ \hline \end{array}$$

$$\begin{array}{r} 3 \\ -1 \\ \hline \end{array}$$

$$\begin{array}{r} 5 \\ -4 \\ \hline \end{array}$$

$$\begin{array}{r} 11 \\ -8 \\ \hline \end{array}$$

$$\begin{array}{r} 3 \\ -2 \\ \hline \end{array}$$

$$\begin{array}{r} 8 \\ -6 \\ \hline \end{array}$$

$$\begin{array}{r} 7 \\ -4 \\ \hline \end{array}$$

10 − 6 =

9 − 5 =

$$\begin{array}{r} 8 \\ -5 \\ \hline \end{array}$$

$$\begin{array}{r} 10 \\ -7 \\ \hline \end{array}$$

4 − 2 =

7 − 5 =

Color Key	If the answer is	Color the space
	1	Red
	2	Green
	3	Blue
	4	Yellow

Add-Up Family Portraits

Children paint a family portrait
with hieroglyphs to write
an addition sentence.

Materials

For each child:

❀ paper grocery bag
❀ brown marker or crayon (optional)
❀ watercolor paints and fine paintbrush
❀ water
❀ paper and pencil
❀ paper towels

1 Introduce this project by explaining hieroglyphs to the class. Ask two children to stand up. Ask the class how many of their classmates are standing. On the chalkboard, write the word *two*. Then ask if there is another way to show this number (2 or **||**).

2 Explain that long ago, before they created an alphabet or numbers for writing, Native Americans such as the Maya used simple pictures to stand for people, animals, and objects. They used the pictures to keep track of how many people were in their nation. They would paint pictures on pieces of bark or animal skins and then count them. Tell your class that, like a Native American nation, they will be inventing symbols— simple pictures—to make a record of their families.

3 On the chalkboard, copy the key shown here. Talk about what each picture represents. Then ask children, "Who do you live with?" On a sheet of paper, have children write down who lives in their home. You may or may not want them to include pets, but explain that a "family" is anyone who lives with them. Some families might include a mom, a dad, a brother or sister, and another family might include a grandmother, an aunt, and two cousins.

4 Ask each child to make a key that explains the pictures they will use to make their family portraits. Point out that the pictures should be simple enough so that everyone can understand them. Then talk about ways children might show the differences between family members—for example, to distinguish between a grown-up and a child.

Making the Family Portraits

1 On the chalkboard, copy the sample family portrait shown here. Talk about the addition sentence it shows. Point out that one type of family member is shown on each line (for example, brothers and sisters). Then have children add with you as you say: $1 + 3 + 1 + 3 = 8$.

2 Give each child a paper grocery bag. Show children how to open up the bag by tearing it down one side. Then have them tear off and discard the bottom of the bag. Explain that the brown paper is like the bark or animal skin some Native Americans once painted on. Tell children to tear off jagged pieces around the edge of the paper to make the "bark" or "leather" look more realistic. (To enhance this effect, let children color the edge of the paper with a brown crayon or marker.)

For background information about the Maya and the hieroglyphs they used, look for *Aztec, Inca & Maya* by Elisabeth Baquedano (Knopf, 1993).

3 Have children write their family's name at the top of the paper. Then have them use a pencil to sketch their pictures on it. Check that their addition sentences are correct.

4 Hand out paints and brushes and let children paint over their sketches.

5 Display children's family portraits on a bulletin board. Invite children to talk with classmates about what makes the different members of their family special.

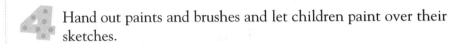

Addition Story Sentences Use children's portraits to make other addition sentences. For example, in the sample shown on page 23, you might ask children to write an addition sentence showing the number of grown-ups added to other family members, or the number of people added to the number of pets. This will help children understand that different combinations of numbers can add up to the same sum. To help children explore other operations, such as subtraction, ask, "How many more pets are there than people?"

Add-Up Class Portraits Help children find out how many family members make up your class's "nation." Together, count up the family members on children's portraits. Make a sign showing the total by writing the number on another piece of torn grocery bag. The sign might say, "Proud First-Grade Nation: 120 Members Strong." (This would be a great activity to do for family nights or parent conference days.)

Soapy Fraction Sculptures

These soapy shapes help children clean up in the fraction department!

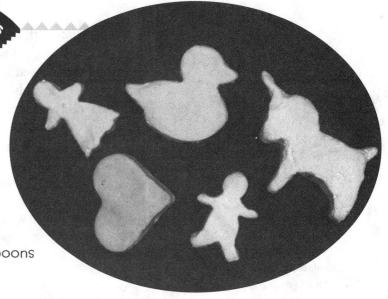

Materials

For each pair of children:

❀ newspaper
❀ smocks
❀ small bowl
❀ $\frac{1}{2}$ cup measure
❀ $\frac{1}{2}$ cup dry soap detergent (preferably Ivory Soap)
❀ $\frac{1}{2}$ cup water in a paper cup
❀ one spoon from a set of measuring spoons
❀ food coloring
❀ paper and pencil
❀ cookie cutters or candy molds (optional)

1 Cover work areas with newspaper and have children put on smocks. Divide the class into pairs. Give a bowl to each pair of children. Tell children that they will be making play dough with soap detergent and water.

2 Measure and place $\frac{1}{2}$ cup of soap detergent in each pair's bowl. Also measure and fill a paper cup with $\frac{1}{2}$ cup of water for each pair. Ask each team if they would like to color their play dough. If so, add a drop of food coloring to their cup of water.

3 Randomly hand out a measuring spoon to each team. Some children will get a $\frac{1}{4}$ teaspoon, others a $\frac{1}{2}$ teaspoon, and so on. Ask children to note the measurement on their spoon.

There's more recipe fun in *The Kids' No-Cook Cookbook* compiled by Beth Goodman (available through Scholastic).

4 Ask each team to estimate how many spoonfuls of water they will need to add so that the mixture will form a ball. Then direct them to add just one spoonful at a time to the bowl. With each spoonful, children should mix the soap and water by squeezing the materials together. Tell the teams to keep track of the number of spoonfuls they use by recording them on paper.

5 Once each team has made a ball of play dough, invite them to shape it into figures, shapes, or whatever they wish. The mixture can also be pressed into cookie cutters, allowed to dry a bit, then carefully poked out. Or children can press the mixture into candy molds, let dry overnight, and then pop out the soap.

6 As a class, discuss the measurements used. Make a chart showing the size of the measuring spoon used by each pair and the number of spoonfuls they used. Help children draw conclusions about the relationship between the size of the spoons and the number used. For example, a group using a $\frac{1}{4}$ teaspoon will use more spoonfuls than a group using a 1 teaspoon measure. Have children write recipes for making their play dough and display them with their soap sculptures.

Team	Size of Spoon	Number of Spoonfuls
Peter and Kim	$\frac{1}{4}$	11
Dylan and Matt	$\frac{1}{4}$	10
Ellen and Mi-Won	$\frac{1}{2}$	5
Adam and Michelle	$\frac{1}{2}$	4
Kathy and Wendy	1	2
José and Philip	1	2

7 Children will enjoy using their Soapy Fraction Sculptures at cleanup time or wrapping them up as handy gifts for family members and friends.

Variation

❀ **SOAPY SNOWMEN** Invite children to make adorable snowmen to give as gifts (skip the food coloring). Have them stack three different-sized balls. While the play dough is still moist, have them poke in arms made of twigs or pieces of pipe cleaner. Then let the sculptures dry to a brilliant white. Using markers, children can fill in the face and add other features. A piece of yarn or ribbon makes a dandy scarf!

Fraction Subtraction Pies

> Children make a fraction pie and use it to model the events in a story.

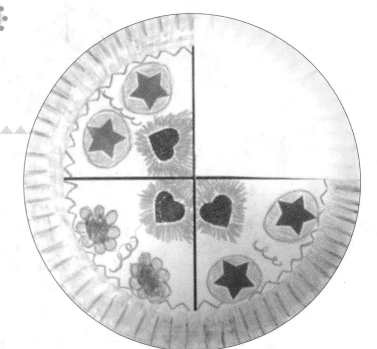

Materials

For each child:

❁ Fraction Pie pattern, page 29
❁ Where Did the Pie Go? story, page 30
❁ two 9-inch paper plates
  (use the lightweight kind that don't have raised rims; these are often the least expensive)
❁ scissors
❁ glue stick
❁ crayons

1 Give each child a copy of the Fraction Pie pattern, two paper plates, scissors, and a glue stick. Let children cut out the Fraction Pie.

2 Show children how to glue the pie pattern to the center of one of the plates. The fluted rim of the plate will stay exposed.

3 Invite children to invent a special kind of pie, encouraging them to be imaginative. Perhaps they'd like to make a gummy candy pie or a popcorn pie. Provide crayons for children to use in designing their pies. Tell them that the edge of the plate is the pie's crust and let them color that, too.

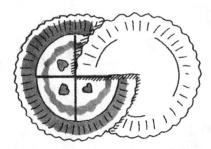 Show children how to stack the paper plates together and then cut through the two plates along the thick black line up to the dot. (Children may need some help doing this.)

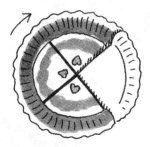 Have them slip the two plates together at the slits. Demonstrate how to turn the decorated plate clockwise to reveal the plain plate. Explain that the plain plate stands for the pan that the pie was baked in.

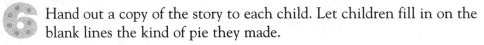

With very young children, you may prefer to write the story on chart paper and read it together with your class.

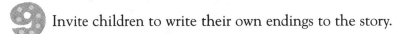 Hand out a copy of the story to each child. Let children fill in on the blank lines the kind of pie they made.

Read the story aloud once, using one of the children's stories. Then read it again, paragraph by paragraph, and ask children to make their pies look the same as the pictures in the story. After reading each paragraph, check to see how children have arranged their plates. Help them to understand that the plain plate (the empty pie pan) represents the amount of pie that was eaten.

Give children additional practice by letting them take turns reading their stories aloud while their classmates use their wheels to model the events of the story.

Invite children to write their own endings to the story.

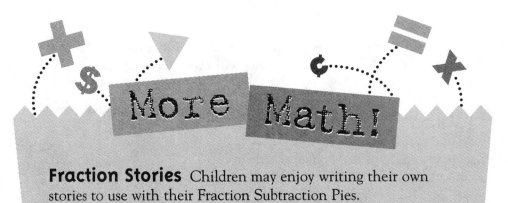

Fraction Stories Children may enjoy writing their own stories to use with their Fraction Subtraction Pies.

Activity adapted from Scholastic's *Math Power* Magazine

Fraction Pie Pattern

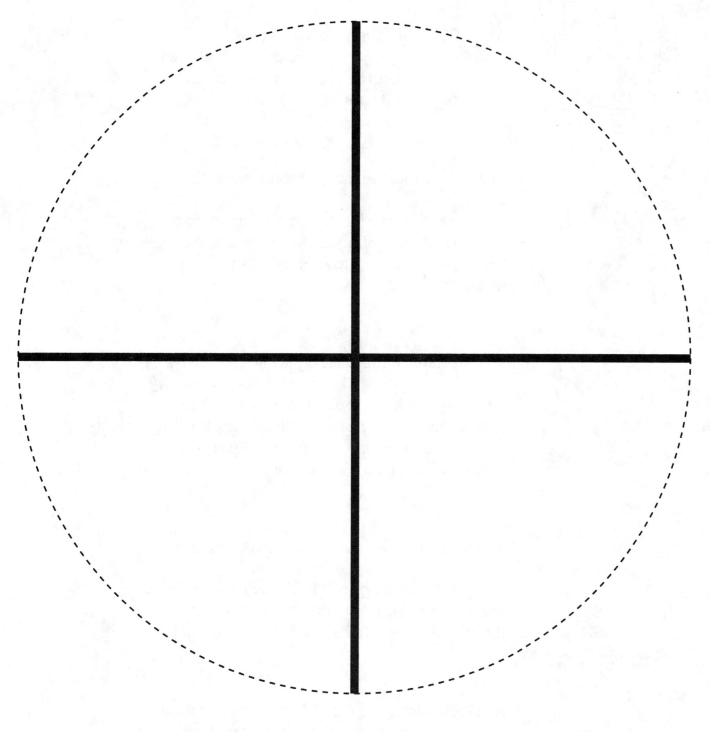

Where Did the Pie Go?

At 12:00 noon, Chef Jeff took his
_____ pie out of the oven.
It looked so pretty. And it smelled so good!
Chef Jeff put it on the windowsill to cool.

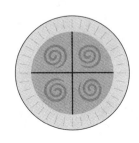

At 3:00, Maria the mailperson walked by.
The _____ pie looked so
pretty. And it smelled so good! Maria hadn't
eaten lunch yet. She was very hungry. So she
took $\frac{1}{4}$ of the pie. Now, $\frac{3}{4}$ of Chef Jeff's pie
was left.

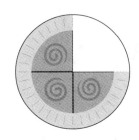

At 6:00, Benny the bulldog walked by. The
_____ pie looked so pretty.
And it smelled so good! It smelled better
than Benny's dog bone. So Benny took a big
bite. He took another $\frac{1}{4}$ of the pie. Now,
only $\frac{1}{2}$ of Chef Jeff's pie was left.

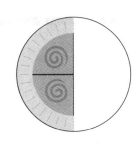

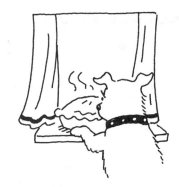

At 9:00, Rosie the raccoon walked by. The
_____ pie looked so pretty.
And it smelled so good. Rosie was ready for a
tasty snack. So she nibbled off another $\frac{1}{4}$ of
the pie. Now, $\frac{3}{4}$ of Chef Jeff's pie was gone!

At 12:00 midnight, Chef Jeff came to check on
his pie. What do you think happened next? Write
the end to the story on the back of this page.

Snapshot Shape Frames

Children focus on geometry by making picture frames in different shapes.

For each child:

❀ Snapshot Shape Frame patterns, pages 34–35 (one per child)

❀ 3- by 5-inch photo

❀ scissors

❀ foam sheet (or heavy construction paper)

❀ $\frac{1}{4}$ of a recycled file folder

❀ glue

❀ paint, markers, stickers, buttons, or ribbon for decorating the frames

❀ clear acetate sheets (optional)

1 Ask children to bring in a 3- by 5-inch photograph of themselves. (In case some children can't bring a photo from home, you can take and develop a picture of each child before this activity is scheduled. Try to photograph children from different perspectives. For example, close-ups, vertical or horizontal shots, and so on.

2 Hold up each of the Snapshot Shape Frames. Ask children to identify the shape of each frame's opening (triangle, circle, rectangle, and square). Place a photograph behind each of the frames, in turn. Ask children how the different-shaped openings change the "look" of the photo. For example, a photo of a child in front of the Magic Castle at Disney World might be enhanced by a triangle-shaped opening, rather than the other shapes. A close-up of a child's face might look good in a frame with a circle-shaped opening. Ask children to decide which frame they would pick to use with the sample photo.

Enlarge the frame patterns to use with larger photographs.

 Ask children to study their photo. What parts do they want to highlight for a viewer? Give children each scissors and their choice of Snapshot Shape Frame. Have children glue the pattern onto either a foam sheet or construction paper. Then have them cut around the outside of the frame and carefully cut out the center. (For easy cutting, have children fold the frame in half and then cut out the center as shown.)

 At this point, let children decorate the front of the frame using paints, markers, glitter, sequins, and other craft materials.

Show children how to make a back for the frame: Have them trace around the frame onto a file folder and cut out the shape.

Give each child three craft sticks to glue to the back of the front piece of the frame as shown. Then children can glue the back of the frame to the craft sticks.

TiP

To prevent smudges on the photo, slip a piece of clear acetate, cut to size, in front of the photo inside the frame.

Show children how to slip the photo inside the frame. (If the photo is too big, help children trim it to fit.)

To display the frames, use the following methods:

🌸 For a tabletop frame, cut a triangle from a scrap of a file folder, fold down one side, and glue to the back of the frame. When the glue is dry, the frame will stand upright on this triangle base.

🌸 To make a hanger, punch a hole at the top of the frame and tie string, yarn, or ribbon to the frame. Or punch a hole in a small piece of cardboard and attach the cardboard to the back of the frame.

9 Display children's creations and encourage them to talk about their frame choices and how the shape enhances their photo.

Variation

🌸 These frames can be made to give away as gifts for any holiday, seasonal celebration, or special occasion. For example, to make a gift for Valentine's Day, children can decorate their frames with paper hearts, scraps of lace, ribbon, or cut-up paper doilies.

Book Gallery

Review familiar shapes with *Brown Rabbit's Shape Book* by Alan Baker (Kingfisher, 1994).

🌸

For more complex shapes, *The Amazing Book of Shapes* by Lydia Sharman (Dorling Kindersley, 1994) brings geometry to life.

🌸

Invite children to look at objects in different ways with Pat Hutchins's *Changes, Changes* (Simon and Schuster, 1971).

🌸

The delightful picture book *Bear in a Square* by Stella Blackstone (Barefoot Books, 1998) invites young readers to search for squares, triangles, circles, and other shapes hidden within the playful illustrations on each page.

Snapshot Shape Frame Patterns

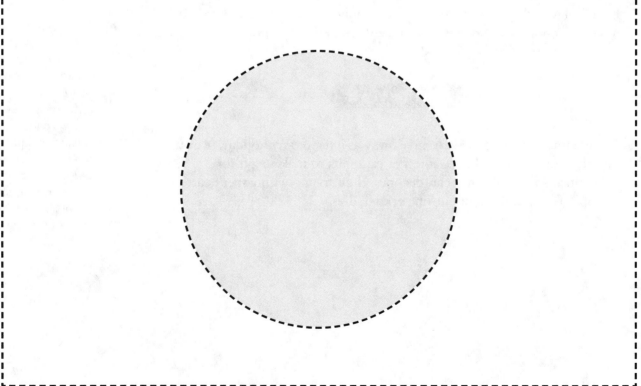

Easy MathART Projects and Activities   Scholastic Professional Books

Snapshot Shape Frame Patterns

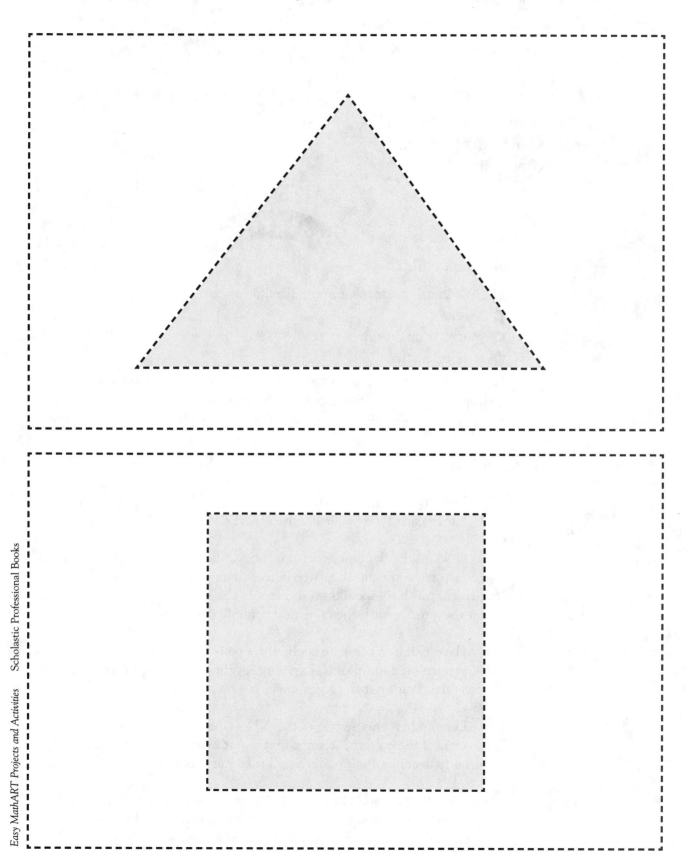

3-D Kiss-mas Ornaments

Children make decorative 3-D boxes that hold clues to geometry (and a treat).

Materials

For each child:

❁ 3-D shape patterns, pages 38–40
❁ scissors
❁ markers or crayons
❁ glue or paste
❁ chocolate kiss candy or another small wrapped candy or toy
❁ tape or stickers (for closing the ornament)
❁ paper clip or ribbon and tape (for hanging the ornament)

Enlarge the patterns if possible. They will be easier for young children to work with.

❁

Before cutting out the patterns, have children paste them to lightweight cardboard (such as a recycled file folder) to make them more durable.

1 Make two copies of each of the patterns and cut them out. Construct one of each type and leave the others flat.

2 Hold up the flat pattern of the cube and explain to children that the picture on the paper is two-dimensional. The two dimensions are length and width. Ask children to identify the shapes on the pattern. Then repeat this process with the cone and pyramid patterns.

3 Have children compare each of the constructions with the flat pattern used to make it. Explain that these shapes are three-dimensional. Point out the length, width, and depth of each.

4 Let children choose one of the 3-D shapes to make. Then give them a copy of the pattern, scissors, crayons or markers, and glue. Invite children to decorate their pattern and then cut it out along the solid lines.

5 Model for children how to fold the patterns along the dotted lines and glue down all but one flap to form a pyramid, cube, or cone. (One side of the shape needs to remain open for inserting the treat.)

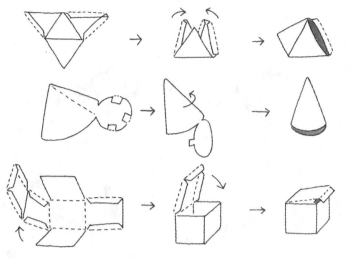

Book Gallery

For more 3-D ornament fun, try *Christmas Origami 1: Tree Ornaments* (Hein International, 1986).

6 Give children each a chocolate kiss, a piece of candy, or a small toy to place inside their ornament. Have them close the last flap and secure with a small piece of tape or a sticker.

7 To hang the ornaments, poke a bent paper clip through one corner or tape on a loop of ribbon.

Variations

Children will enjoy decorating and filling these geometric ornaments with goodies for any occasion:

❀ **HALLOWEEN** Decorate ornaments with orange and black pumpkins, witches, and cats. Include a trick (a Halloween riddle or joke) and a treat (a piece of candy, a balloon, or a sticker).

❀ **VALENTINE'S DAY** Let children decorate their ornaments with red and white hearts. Fill them with a Valentine's message and a heart-shaped piece of chocolate.

More Math!

3-D Shape Scavenger Hunt Challenge children to find everyday objects that come in different three-dimensional shapes (cone: ice cream cones; tops of mustard dispensers; cylinder: metal cans, oatmeal and bread crumb containers; cubes: ice cubes, square notepads that come in cubes).

Fill 'Em Up! Introduce the concept of volume to your class by asking children to estimate how many spoonfuls of unpopped corn kernels it will take to fill each of the different ornaments. As a class, fill each ornament with corn and compare estimates with results. Then repeat the activity with popped corn. How do the results differ?

Pyramid Pattern

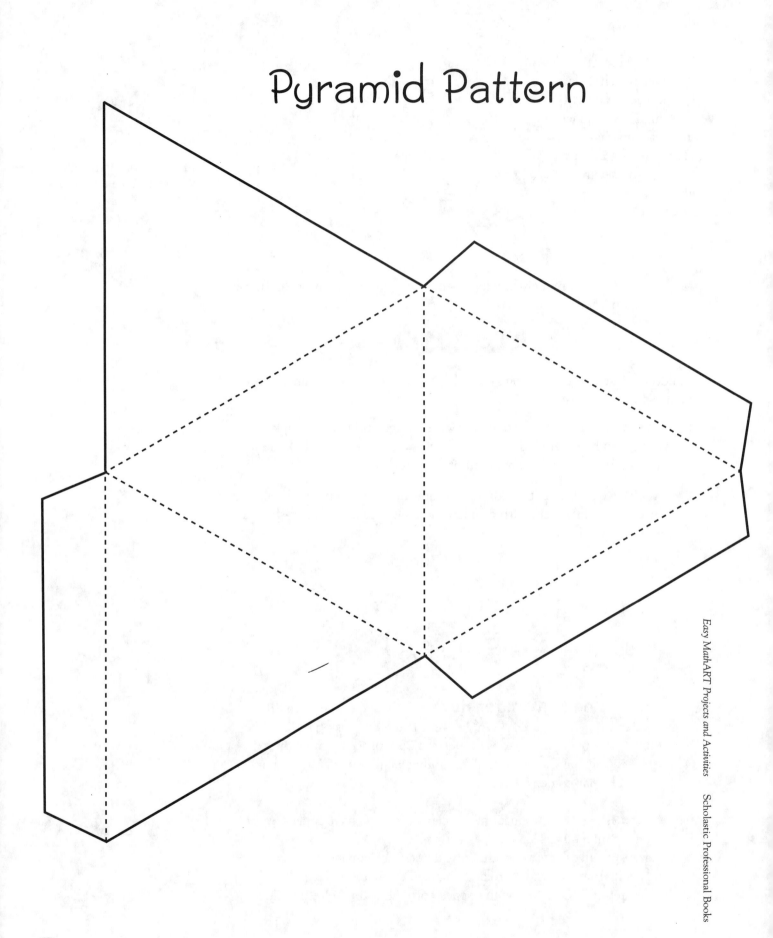

Easy MathART Projects and Activities   Scholastic Professional Books

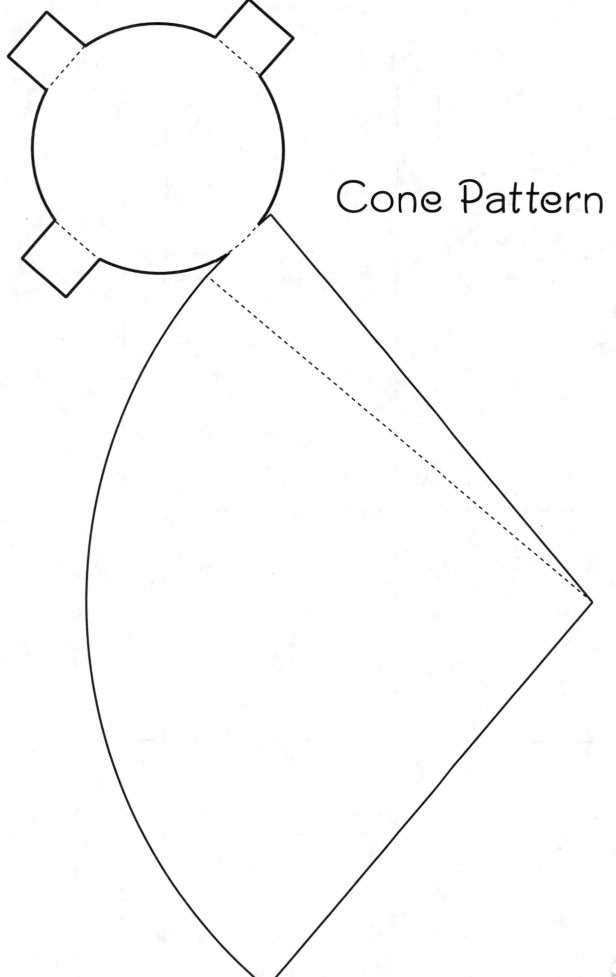

Cone Pattern

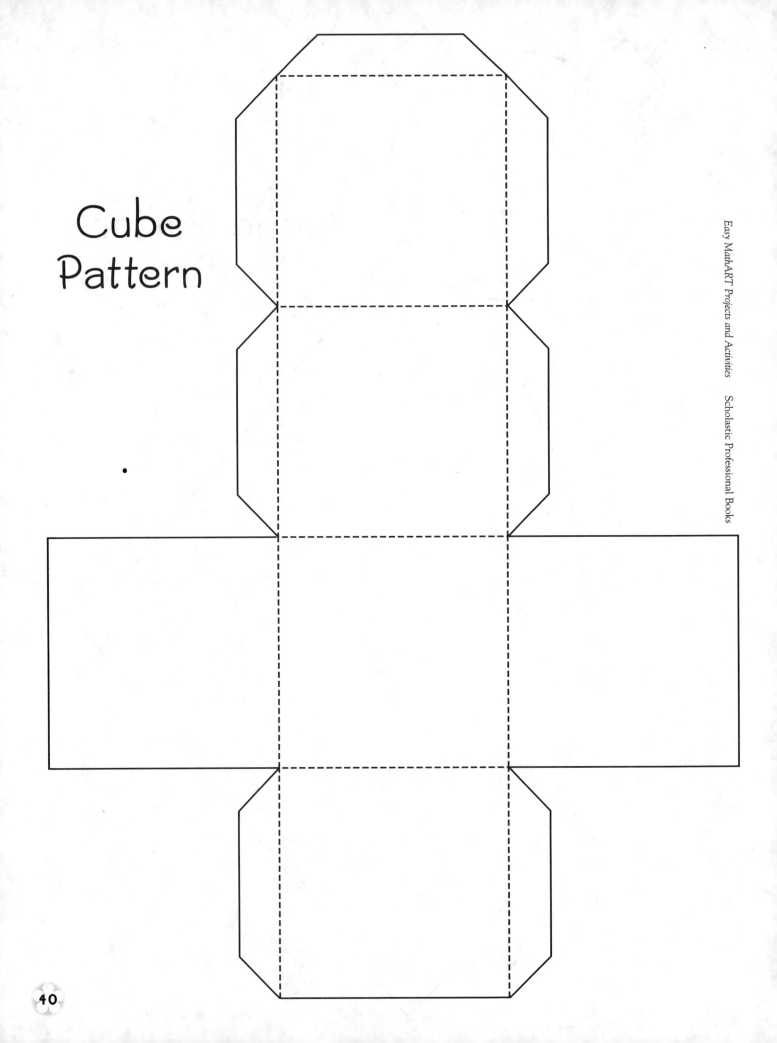

Cube
Pattern

Easy MathART Projects and Activities   Scholastic Professional Books

Heart-Filled Valentines

> Children explore estimation and volume by filling a Valentine with sweet hearts!

Materials

For each child:

- 2 small heart-shaped or round doilies
- 1 foot red, white, or pink curling ribbon
- small candy conversation hearts (number will vary)
- paper and pencil
- hole punch (optional)

Ahead of Time

If the doilies you use have very small holes, you may want to use a hole punch to make larger holes around the edges. Children will be threading ribbon through these holes.

1 Divide the class into groups. Give each child two doilies and a piece of ribbon. Have children knot one end of the ribbon. Then show them how to sew together the two doilies. They do this by first lining up the doilies, then weaving the unknotted end of the ribbon in and out of the holes around the edges of the doilies. Have them leave a wide opening at the top.

Book Gallery

Fun and funny poems by Jack Prelutsky give children an insight into all aspects of this heartfelt holiday in *It's Valentine's Day* (Scholastic, 1986).

2 Pass out five small candy hearts to each child. Ask: "How many hearts do you think you will need to fill your heart packet and still be able to sew it closed?" Ask children to record their estimates.

3 Tell children to take the number of hearts they estimate will fill the heart. As children fill the hearts, ask them how close they think their estimates will come to the actual number.

4 Ask how many chose too many hearts. How many children chose too few? How many children think they chose just the right number?

5 Children can record their final number, then sew the tops of the hearts closed, make a bow, and cut off any excess.

6 As a class, discuss the estimates and results. Write children's figures on the chalkboard. Ask children to describe their estimating methods. Together, conclude why some estimates were more accurate than others.

More Math!

Valentines With Big Hearts Repeat the activity using large candy conversation hearts (or another candy that comes in larger pieces). Ask children to draw conclusions about how the size of the candies relates to the number needed to fill the hearts. (The larger the candies, the fewer pieces needed.)

Pipe-Cleaner Pals

Children make Pipe-Cleaner Pals to explore nonstandard measurement.

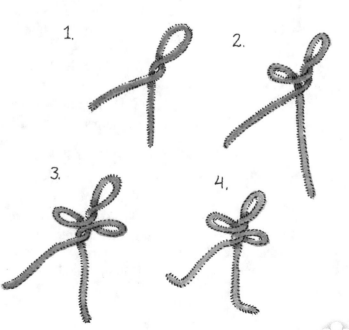

Materials

For each group:

❀ 12-inch pipe cleaners, in different colors
❀ Measure Hunt! Chart, page 45
❀ ruler
❀ yardstick

1 Divide the class into groups of four. Give each child a pipe cleaner. Ask children to bend their pipe cleaner to make different shapes and objects.

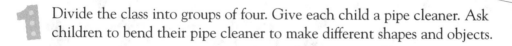

2 Let children share the shapes they made. Then follow the drawings here to show children how to form a Pipe-Cleaner Pal.

1.

2.

3 Using fresh pipe cleaners, let each child make three Pipe-Cleaner Pals. Ask each group to compare their Pals. They should each be about the same size.

3.

4.

4 Give each group a copy of the chart. Ask: "How many Pipe-Cleaner Pals long is your chart?" Let children practice laying their pals end to end to measure the paper.

Book Gallery

How many ways can you measure a dog? Readers find out in *Measuring Penny* by Loreen Leedy (Henry Holt, 1987).

5 Explain that each group should work together to generate a list of classroom objects to add to the list on the chart, estimate how many Pipe-Cleaner Pals long or tall the object is, and record their estimates. Then they should take turns using the group's Pipe-Cleaner Pals to check their estimates. Discuss strategies for rounding up or down to the nearest whole measure.

6 Once the groups have finished measuring, have them compare their estimates with their results. Then ask: "What was easy about measuring with your Pals? What was hard? Can you think of a way to measure big objects with your Pals?" Show children a ruler and a yardstick. Point out the inch and foot increments. Discuss reasons they might use different measuring tools (inches are useful for measuring smaller objects; a yardstick is easier to use for larger objects).

7 Challenge each group to find a way to make a larger measuring tool using their Pals. Children might make a chain by linking their Pals together. (An easy way to do this is to bend the foot of one around the head of another.) Or they might glue the Pals, end to end, onto a long strip of cardboard.

8 Let children use their new tool to remeasure the objects on their chart. Do their measurements differ?

Pipe-Cleaner-Pal Graphs Use the Pals for graphing. On a bulletin board, tack up sentence strips on which you've written questions such as "Do You Have a Pet?" or "Do You Like Pizza?" Also tack up index cards labeled "Yes" and "No." Provide pushpins and let children respond to the question by hanging a Pal under the appropriate card. Have children link the Pals together as described in step 7 above. To analyze the data, have children compare the lengths of the chains.

Pipe-Cleaner-Pal Manipulatives Use the Pals as manipulatives to represent the children in your class. For each class member, put one Pal in a basket. Ask children to use the Pals to come up with ways for the class to line up in two equal groups, for example, or in rows of three, four, or five. You can also ask children to use the Pals to solve math problems, such as "How many children are in class today, if three are out sick?"

Names _____

Measure Hunt! Chart

Things We Measured	Estimate	Actual Measurement
1 This chart		
2 Pencil		
3 Chalkboard		
4 _____ (name of child)		
5		
6		
7		
8		
9		
10		

Cuckoo Clocksicles

Children create cuckoo clocks for time-telling adventures!

Materials

For each child:

❀ Clock patterns, page 49
❀ half of a recycled file folder
❀ glue stick
❀ scissors
❀ marker
❀ crayons or colored markers
❀ hole punch (to share)
❀ craft stick or unsharpened pencil
❀ brass fastener
❀ tape
❀ piece of yarn, about 12 inches long (optional)
❀ 2 large beads (optional)

Making the Cuckoo Clocksicle

1 Review the different parts of an analog clock. Depending on the level of your students, explain that a clock has 12 numbers, one number for each hour in the day. The short hand points to the hour, the long hand points to the minute. There are 60 minutes in every hour. Review A.M. and P.M.

2 Give each child a copy of the clock patterns page, a glue stick, and half of a file folder. Tell children to glue the pattern page to the half folder and then cut out each of the five pieces. Have them punch a hole through the dot on each clock hand.

Have children use a marker to trace each of the numbers on the clock face. Then invite them to decorate the clock, the two clock hands, and the cuckoo strip.

4 Have children assemble the clock as shown.

✿ Put the minute hand and then the hour hand on top of the clock face.

✿ Use a pencil point to make a hole in the clock face, then attach the clock hands with a brass fastener.

5 Show children how to tape the crosspiece to the back of the clock as shown. Then have them slide the cuckoo strip, colored side down, under the crosspiece. Also have them tape a craft stick or a pencil to the back of the clock as shown.

6 To make the clock's weighted cords (optional), children can tie a bead to each end of a piece of yarn and tape the yarn to the back of their Clocksicle as shown.

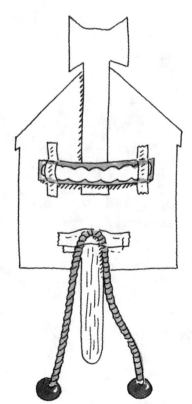

Using the Cuckoo Clocksicles

1 Review significant times of the day: the start of the school day, snack time, lunch, recess, and so on.

2 Position the clock hands on your Clocksicle to a particular hour, such as 3 o'clock. Ask children to read the time and then adjust their clocks to match yours. When everyone's clock is set correctly, invite children to hold up their Clocksicles and slide their cuckoo up and down three times to mark the hour. At the same time, have them say, "It's 3 o'clock. Cuckoo! Cuckoo! Cuckoo!" (Children say "Cuckoo" as many times as the hour on the clock.)

3 Let children practice setting their Clocksicles to different times, continuing in this fashion. Use examples that begin early in the day and end later, so that their Clocksicles run clockwise. Explain that this is how a real clock moves.

4 At different times of the day, such as snack, recess, or gym, ask children to use the classroom clock to read the time and set their Clocksicles accordingly. You can also use the clocks to have children count how many hours until a particular activity, or until the end of the school day.

More Math!

Digital Time Once children are adept at telling analog time, let them practice recording digital times in their math journals, using words and numbers (for example, two o'clock and 2:00).

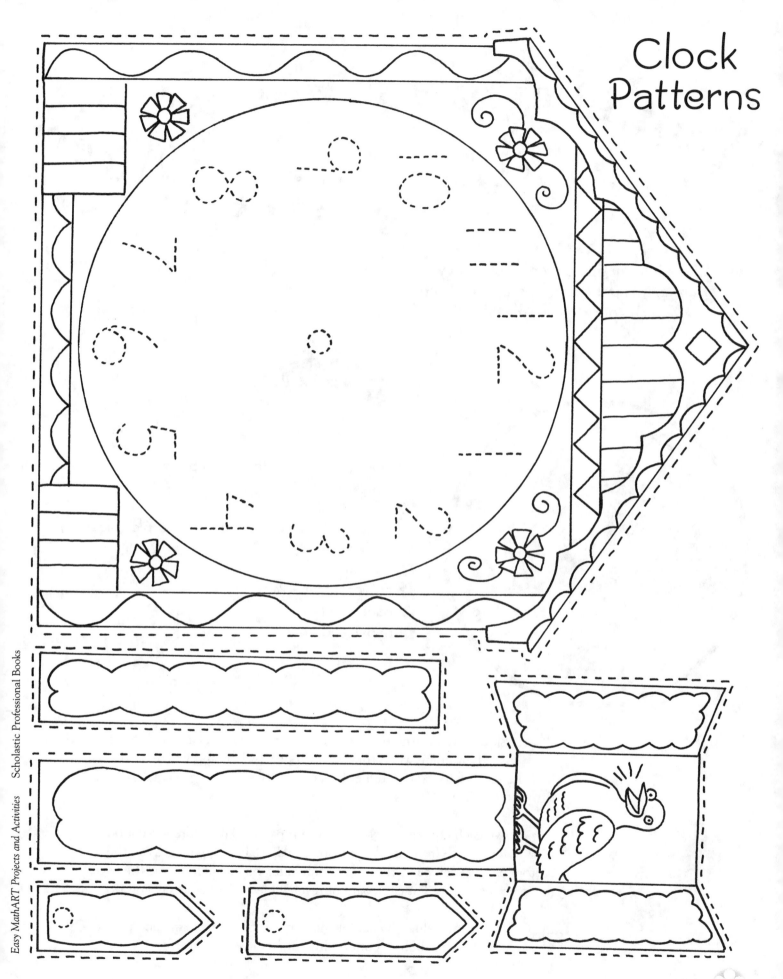

Clock Patterns

Tooth Fairy Money-Tree Wheels

Children make "cents" of money amounts left by the Tooth Fairy when they spin Money-Tree Wheels.

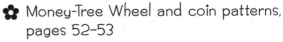
Materials

For each child:

- ❁ Money-Tree Wheel and coin patterns, pages 52–53
- ❁ scissors
- ❁ lightweight cardboard or recycled file folder (optional)
- ❁ glue stick
- ❁ crayons or markers
- ❁ paper fastener
- ❁ paper and pencil

1 Ask children to share "tooth fairy" stories. Ask: "Does the tooth fairy visit their home when they lose a tooth? When and where do they find the tooth fairy's gift?" Tell children that they are going to make Tooth Fairy Money-Tree Wheels.

2 Give each child a copy of the pattern pages. Tell children to cut out the Money Tree front and back along the dotted lines, setting aside the bottom part of each page. (For added durability, have children glue the pages to a piece of lightweight cardboard or reycled file folder before cutting.)

3 Review the values of each of the coins at the bottom of each pattern page. Tell children to cut out any nine coins for their tree.

4 On the back of the Money Tree, have children glue the coins over the squares. They can use a crayon lightly to shade the coins, if they like. If they do this, have them color each kind of coin a different color: pennies, red; nickels, blue; and so on.

Book Gallery

What is money? Who were the first people to use it? These and other questions are answered in Neale S. Godfrey's *The Kids' Money Book* (Scholastic, 1996).

Share Caren Holtzman's *A Quarter From the Tooth Fairy* (Scholastic, 1996) for a clever story about a boy, his quarter, and the different combinations that add up to 25.

5 Help children cut out the three windows on the front of their Money Tree. To cut out the windows easily, loosely curve or bend the paper in half at a right angle to the line to be cut. To start the cut, snip along the dotted line. Reopen the paper and insert the tip of the scissors into the slit. Carefully finish cutting along the dotted line. Children may then color their trees, if desired.

6 Have children place the front of the Money Tree on top of the back, poke a paper fastener through the dot in the center of each wheel, and spread open the ends of the fastener.

7 Ask children to turn the wheel until a coin appears in each window. Ask: "What coins did the Tooth Fairy leave on your tree?" Then ask: "How much money did the Tooth Fairy leave?" Let children take turns holding up their wheels, naming the coins that appear in the windows and giving the sum. Let classmates check each other.

8 Continue in this manner, having children turn their wheels until three new coins appear in the window. Then have them add up the value of these coins. (Each child's tree will have three different combinations of coins.) Let chilDen record these values in their math journals. As an added challenge, ask children to figure out the total value of the coins on their tree.

9 For more practice, have children trade trees and record their money combinations and totals in their math journals.

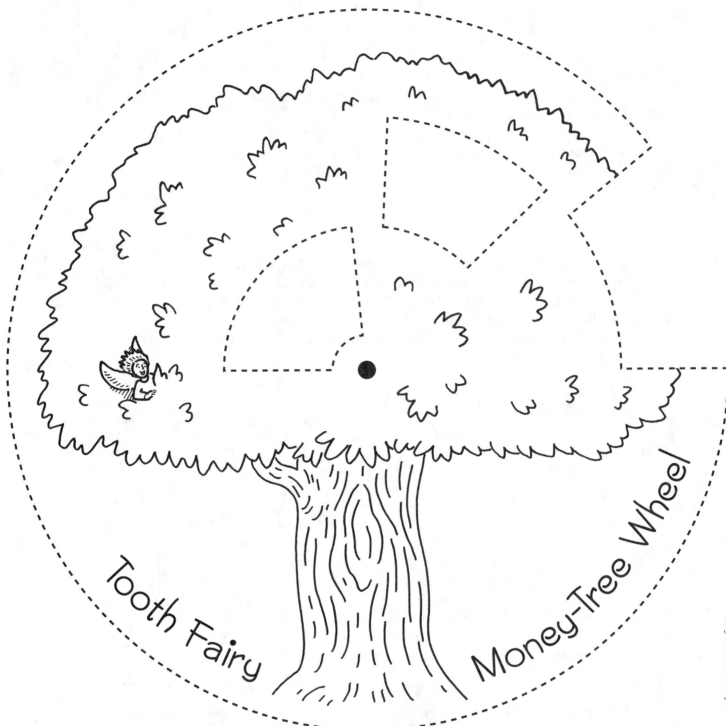

Tooth Fairy

Money-Tree Wheel

Money-Tree Wheel
(Top)

Easy MathART Projects and Activities   Scholastic Professional Books

Money-Tree Wheel
(Bottom)

Harvest Corncob Patterns

Celebrate the harvest season by creating a cornucopia of colorful, patterned corncobs!

Materials

For each child:

✿ Indian corn (optional)
✿ Corncob pattern, page 58
✿ lightweight cardboard (recycled file folders work well)
✿ glue
✿ scissors
✿ plastic sandwich bag
✿ unpopped corn kernels in different colors, or pieces of colorful ball-shaped cereal
✿ paper plate
✿ two 4- by 7-inch pieces of yellow or gold tissue or twisted paper ribbon (available at craft stores)

1 If you are able to get Indian corn, pass around samples. Let children observe the different color patterns on each ear.

2 Give each child a a paper plate and a plastic sandwich bag filled with dried popcorn kernels in different colors. Review what a pattern is (something that repeats over and over). Then ask children to take from their bags several kernels in two different colors and arrange them in a pattern on their plate. Let children describe the different patterns they made (1 green/1 blue/1 green/1 blue; 2 green/1 blue/2 green/1 blue, and so on). Have children return the kernels to their bags.

3 Give each child one corncob pattern. Have them glue the pattern onto a piece of cardboard and then cut it out.

4 Tell children to use the kernels to make a colored pattern on their corncob. You might suggest that children first sort their kernels by color on their plates. Let children experiment making different patterns. When they have decided on a pattern they would like to keep, have them glue the kernels to the corncob in their chosen pattern.

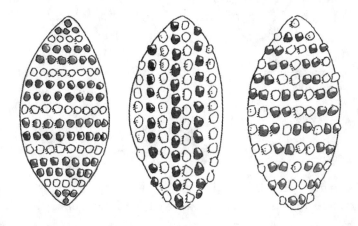

5 To make the cob look like a real ear of corn, give each child two pieces of tissue or twisted paper ribbon. Show children how to overlap the pieces and twist them together at one end. Then they glue the corncob inside and curl back back the "husk" to reveal the kernels.

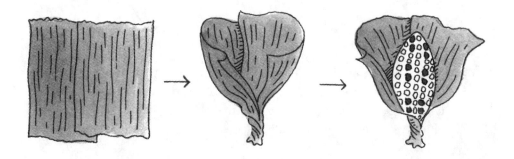

Variation

❁ Instead of gluing the kernels to the corncob patterns, children can make corncob-shaped pieces of clay (either flat or three-dimensional) and then press the kernels, in patterns, into the clay.

Book Gallery

Share *Corn Is Maize: The Gift of the Indians* by Aliki (Harper, 1976) with your class to help them learn about the important role corn has played for people around the world.

If you use this activity as a tie-in for Kwanzaa, read *Seven Candles for Kwanzaa* by Andrea Davis Pinkney (Dial, 1993) for a touching rendition of the traditions of this holiday.

For wonderful illustrations of woven patterns, invite children to look at Debbi Chocolate's *Kente Colors* (Walker & Co., 1996).

More Math!

Corn and Mkekas for Kwanzaa During Kwanzaa, ears of corn are placed on a woven mat called an mkeka, one ear for each child in a family. Let children make simple woven patterned mats, following the directions below, and place on them the correct number of ears of corn to represent their family. Help children make name labels to identify their mats.

❖ For each mat, make four 2- by 9-inch construction paper strips in two different colors. Then fold a piece of 9- by 12-inch construction paper in half the short way. Draw a line about $1\frac{1}{2}$ inches from the edge of the open end. This is where children should stop cutting.

❖ Starting at the fold and about $1\frac{1}{2}$ inches from one side, cut a straight line through the paper to the line. Repeat to make three more slits in the paper.

❖ Open the paper and spread it flat. Weave the first paper strip through the slits, weaving over and under them. Continue weaving, alternating the colors, until the mat is filled. Then glue the edges of the strips in place.

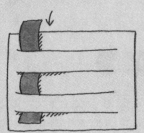 

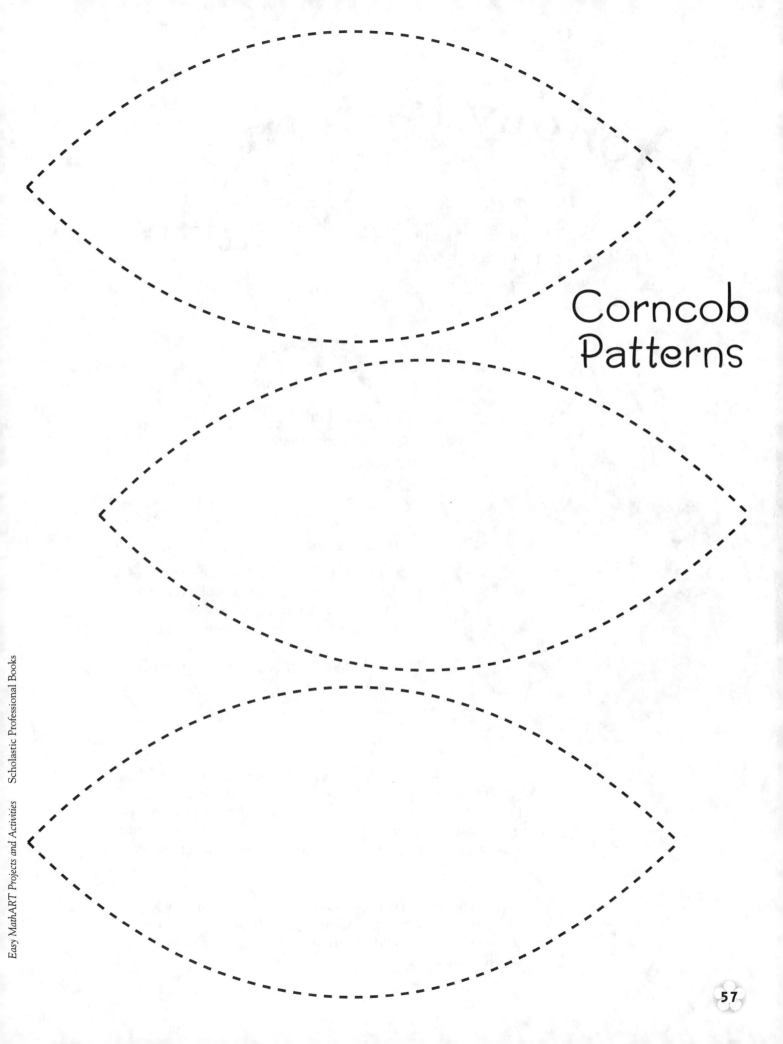

Corncob
Patterns

Holiday Pattern Wreaths

Children explore different kinds of patterns when they design festive winter holiday wreaths.

Materials

For each child:

* large paper plate
* scissors
* half a sheet of green tissue paper
* glue

For each group:

* tray filled with pattern pieces such as wrapped candy, beads, colorful dried beans, fun-shaped erasers, pipe cleaners, small holiday balls, pieces of garland, and paper snowflakes, bells, and other shapes created with craft hole punches

1 Divide the class into small groups. Give each group a trayful of different kinds of pattern pieces (see Materials). Tell each group to sort the objects on their tray. Ask a volunteer from each group to describe their groupings. On the chalkboard, make a list of different ways children sorted the items (by color, type, shape, texture, and other characteristics).

2 Tell each group to make a pattern using some of their objects. Then ask groups to swap places. Challenge each group to try to guess another group's pattern and to continue it. Discuss the different kinds of patterns children made.

3 Give each child a paper plate and scissors. Ask children to cut out the center of the plate. (It's not important if the center is not perfectly round.) Children may need help making the first cut.

4 Hand out the colored tissue paper and show children how to tear up pieces of the tissue and gently bunch them up. Show them how to glue these bunches of tissue to the paper plate. Let children follow this process to cover their plate with tissue.

5 Invite children to decorate their wreath with some of the objects on their tray. Ask them to create a pattern as they place the items around the wreath. Remind them to think about the different ways the objects could be sorted and to use this information as they plan their patterns. Encourage them to explore other ways to create patterns (for example, by position and quantity).

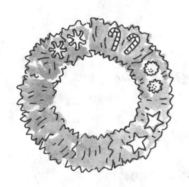

6 When children are satisfied with their patterns, ask them to glue the items to their wreath. When the glue is dry, help them punch holes in the plate as shown. Give each child a piece of ribbon or yarn to string through the holes. They can simply knot the ends, and the wreaths are ready to hang!

Book Gallery

Share Edna Barth's Holly, Reindeer, and Colored Lights (Clarion Books, 1971) and Christmas Time by Gail Gibbons (Holiday House, 1988), two good books to use for discussing the different holiday traditions people celebrate.

Variations

Wreaths can be made to celebrate any holiday or special event just by changing the materials you used.

✿ THANKSGIVING Use orange tissue paper, leaves, acorns, pinecones, and twigs.

✿ VALENTINE'S DAY Use pink and red tissue paper, candy conversation hearts, and paper hearts.

✿ SPRING Use pastel-colored tissue paper, flower and animal stickers, and jelly beans.

More Math!

Pattern-Print Paper Let children continue their exploration of patterns by making holiday gift wrap. Let children dip precut sponges in paint (a few colors is all children need) and use them to make prints on large pieces of craft paper. (These sponges come in many different shapes and are available by the bagful at arts and crafts stores.) A fun way to do this activity is to pair up children and have them take turns starting and continuing each other's patterns on the same piece of paper. Or one child can print a pattern but leave out one item in the sequence. Partners try to guess and fill in the missing print.

Costume-Combo Flip Books

On Halloween, or anytime, children will flip for the wacky costume combinations they can create!

Materials

For each child:

❀ Costume-Combo patterns, pages 63–64
❀ crayons or markers
❀ scissors
❀ stapler

1 Give each child a copy of each of the pattern pages, crayons, and scissors. Ask children to identify each of the four costume characters. Then invite children to color the pictures.

2 Tell children to cut out each page along the dotted lines. When cutting the inner flaps, make sure they don't cut all the way through the pages. They should cut only up to the thin solid line. Children then stack together the pages and staple as shown.

Book Gallery

Share *The Perfect Match* by Wayne Anderson (Dorling Kindersley, 1995) with your class. This interactive book is a great example of the type of book children make in this activity.

❀

Enjoy a rollicking good time with the trick-or-treaters in Jack Prelutsky's delightful poetry collection *It's Halloween* (Scholastic, 1986).

3 Model for students how to use the flip book to make different costume combinations. Hold up the book, without turning any of the pages. Explain that the three parts of the baseball player, for example, make up one combination. Then fold back the page with the ballerina's head to reveal the clown's face, for example. Explain that this is another costume combination. Ask children what name they might give to this costume character.

4 Give children plenty of time to fold back the top, middle, or bottom pages of their books to create different costume combinations. Ask them to record in their math journals the different combinations they make. Children may also enjoy giving their costume characters new names.

5 On the chalkboard, make a list of the different combinations children made. By the way, there are 64 possible combinations in all!

Costume-Combo Patterns

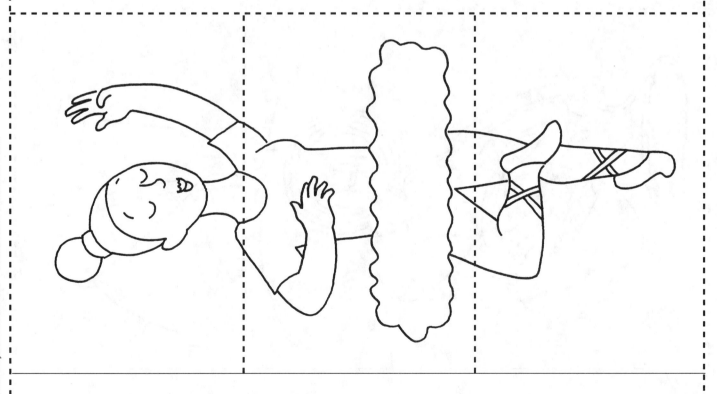

Costume-Combo Patterns

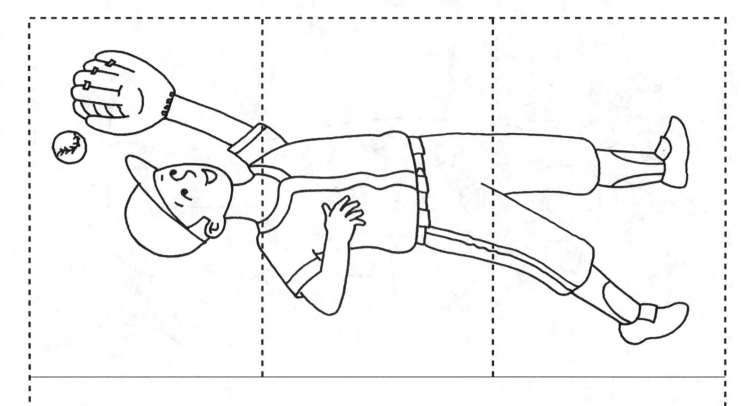

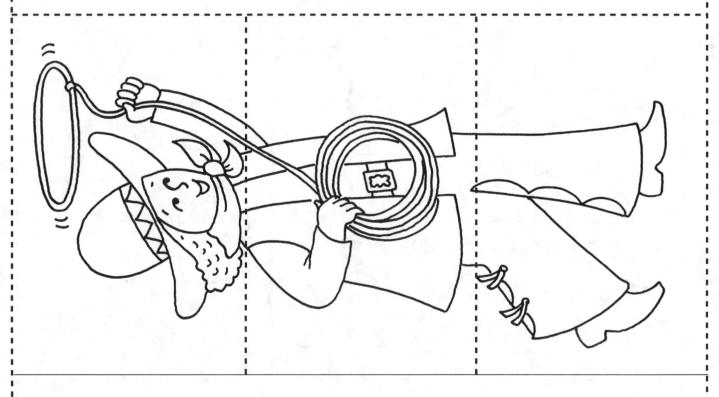

Easy MathART Projects and Activities Scholastic Professional Books